Mars
The Red Planet

By Lincoln James

Clifton Park - Halfmoon Public Library
475 Moe Road
Clifton Park, New York 12065

Gareth Stevens
Publishing

Please visit our Web site, www.garethstevens.com. For a free color catalog of all our high-quality books, call toll free 1-800-542-2595 or fax 1-877-542-2596.

Library of Congress Cataloging-in-Publication Data

James, Lincoln.
  Mars : the red planet / Lincoln James.
     p. cm. — (Our solar system)
  Includes bibliographical references and index.
  ISBN 978-1-4339-3825-2 (pbk)
  ISBN 978-1-4339-3826-9 (6-pack)
  ISBN 978-1-4339-3824-5 (lib binding)
  1. Mars (Planet)—Juvenile literature. I. Title.
  QB641.J34 2011
  523.43—dc22
                                           2010000488
First Edition

Published in 2011 by
Gareth Stevens Publishing
111 East 14th Street, Suite 349
New York, NY 10003

Designer: Daniel Hosek
Editor: Greg Roza

Photo credits: Cover, p. 1 © Photodisc; pp. 5, 7 Shutterstock.com; p. 9 (Phobos) NASA/JPL/University of Arizona; p. 9 (Deimos) NASA/JPL-caltech/University of Arizona; p. 11 NASA/JPL/Cornell; p. 13 Space Frontiers/Hulton Archive/Getty Images; pp. 15 (main image), 17 NASA/Getty Images; p. 15 (inset) NASA/Viking Project; p. 19 AFP/Getty Images; p. 21 NASA/Pat Rawlings, SAIC.

Printed in the United States of America

CPSIA compliance information: Batch #CS10GS: For further information contact Gareth Stevens, New York, New York at 1-800-542-2595.

Contents

Boldface words appear in the glossary.

Welcome to Mars!

In our **solar system**, Mars is the fourth planet from the sun. Mars is called the red planet because it looks red from Earth.

Our Solar System

Neptune

Uranus

Saturn

Jupiter

Mars

Earth

Venus

Mercury

sun

5

Days and Years

A day on Mars is about 40 minutes longer than a day on Earth. A year on Mars is about 687 days. This is how long it takes Mars to go around the sun once.

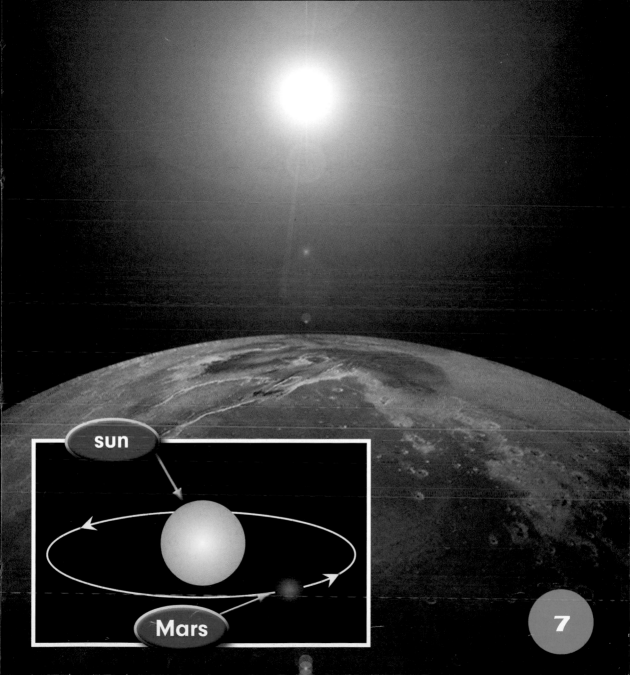

sun

Mars

The Moons of Mars

Mars has two tiny moons called Phobos (FOH-bohs) and Deimos (DAY-mohs). They are not round like our moon. Phobos is larger than Deimos.

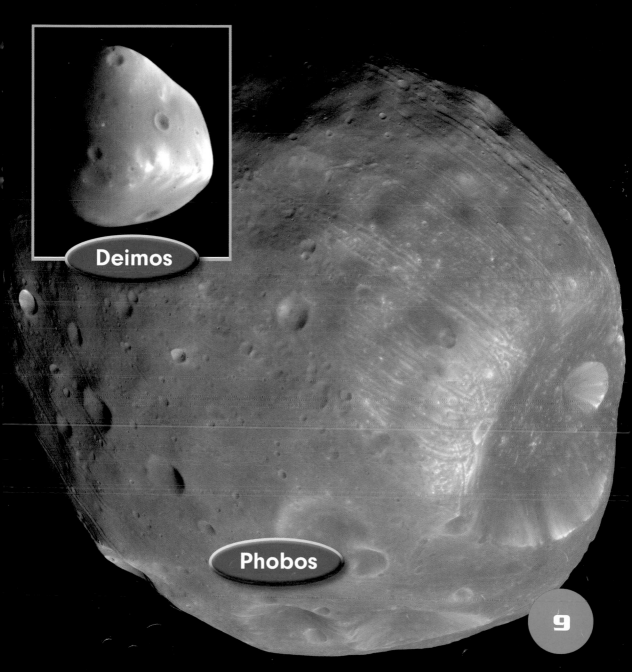

Deimos

Phobos

9

The Land on Mars

Mars is rocky and sandy. Mars looks red because of the iron in the sand. Sometimes Mars has dust storms. The dust storms can cover the whole planet!

11

Mars has many mountains and valleys. The tallest **volcano** in our solar system is on Mars. The volcano is three times taller than Earth's tallest mountain!

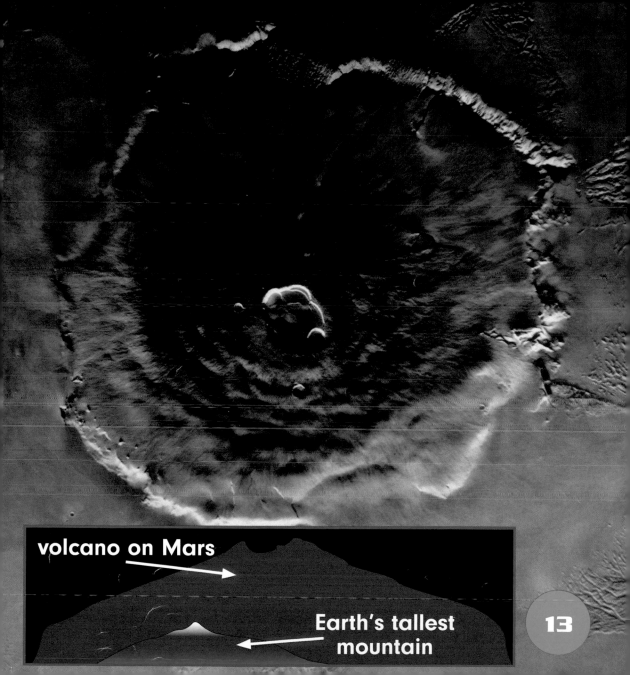

volcano on Mars

Earth's tallest mountain

Mars also has many **canyons**. The largest canyon in our solar system is on Mars. The canyon is about four times deeper than Earth's deepest canyon!

canyon

15

Water on Mars

Mars has ice at its **poles**. It also has ice under the ground. Scientists think the planet may once have been covered with water.

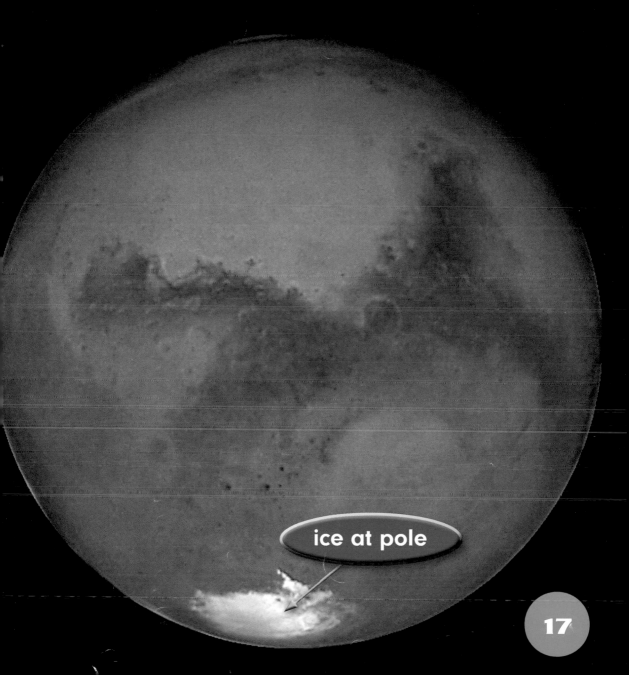

ice at pole

Life on Mars?

Some scientists think there was once life on Mars. Scientists have sent many **probes** to Mars to learn more about the red planet.

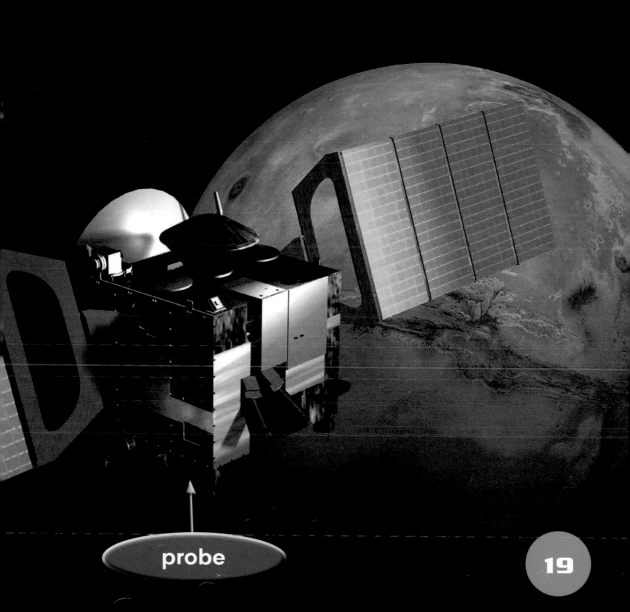

probe

Someday, **astronauts** may visit Mars. Some scientists think people could even live there someday! We will keep studying Mars for years to come.

Glossary

astronaut: someone who travels and works in space

canyon: a deep valley with steep sides

pole: the northernmost or southernmost part of a planet

probe: an unmanned spaceship

solar system: the sun and all the space objects that orbit it, including the planets and their moons

volcano: an opening in a planet's surface through which hot, liquid rock sometimes flows

For More Information

Books

Simon, Seymour. *Destination: Mars.* New York, NY: HarperCollins, 2004.

Wimmer, Teresa. *Mars.* Mankato, MN: Creative Education, 2008.

Web Sites

Mars

www.kidsastronomy.com/mars.htm

Read about Mars and see images and diagrams of the red planet.

Mars Exploration Program: Welcome to Mars

marsprogram.jpl.nasa.gov/funzone_flash.html

Learn about Mars with fun, educational games and activities.

Index

About the Author

Lincoln James is a retired aerospace engineer and amateur astronomer living in St. Augustine, Florida. He enjoys building miniature rockets with his four sons and taking family trips to the Kennedy Space Center to watch space shuttle launches.